Friends
Finding and Keeping Them

KAREN DOCKREY

9/30/85

Johnnie,

Genuine friends like you are such a treasure. Thanks for your consistent and thoughtful caring. Looking forward to a long and growing friendship with you + Phyllis

Karen

BROADMAN PRESS
Nashville, Tennessee

ISBN: 0-8054-5343-1
4253-43

Dewey Decimal Classification: 177
Subject Heading: FRIENDSHIP
Library of Congress Catalog Number: 85-12783

Printed in the United States of America

Library of Congress Cataloging in Publication Data

Dockrey, Karen, 1955-
Friends: finding and keeping them.

Summary: Addresses from a Christian perspective questions and concerns about friendship, including "First Steps Toward Friendship" and "The Courage to Be Myself."
Includes index.
1. Friendship—Moral and ethical aspects—Juvenile literature. [1. Friendship. 2. Christian life]
I. Title.
BJ1533.F8D62 1985 241'.676 85-12783
ISBN 0-8054-5343-1 (pbk.)

To Emily and Sarah
with prayers for their lifelong friendship

Acknowledgments

Thanks to the youth of Parkwood Baptist Church, Annandale, Virginia, for giving many of the words in this book; and to the youth of Parkside Baptist Church, Columbus, Indiana, for sharing their friendship problems and solutions; and to Bill, Rita, Norma, and Sally for loving me with the friendship skills described in this book.

Contents

Contents

Why Can't I Have Friends Like Everybody Else?

Other people meet friends so easily! Their friendships seem so comfortable and problem free! Why can't I have friends like everybody else?

We believe that friendship comes naturally. Many parts of it do. But making and keeping friends are skills, and like other skills, they improve with practice and knowledge.

People who are comfortable making friends have simply learned how. They have known people who modeled good friendship, have taken classes, have talked with people about their friendships, have read books, and have practiced what they learn. Much of this learning came without realizing it. Other skills came through hard work and practice.

You can become one of those people who is comfortable meeting and growing close to friends. You can understand and be understood, deal with problems, and enjoy your friendships. You can develop your friendship skills.

The first step is to make a commitment to do so. Then try some of the following:

- Read this book and others like it.
- Find people who have good friendships. Notice what they do and imitate their actions. Soon friendship skills will come naturally to you.

• Put yourself in your friend's position. What are her needs? How can you meet them?

• Take a class on communication, peer counseling, or another friendship skill.

• Pay attention to yourself. What do you do well? Poorly? Cultivate good friendship skills and weed out friendship destroyers. Find the courage to improve!

• Study what God and the Bible say about friendship. You'll find many friendship verses in the Bible.

• Pray for God's guidance and strength. He created friendship. He knows best how to find and keep it.

Why a book on friendship?

1. We need friends.
2. We want to improve our friendships.
3. There are ways to build better friendships.

This book explains some of these ways. It gives tips on how to get started in a friendship, ways to keep a good relationship going, how to conquer problems, ways to communicate, how to be yourself, ways to help friends with problems, and much more.

Each chapter in this book deals with a portion of friendship. You might begin by reading the chapter that deals with your concern. But because each chapter builds on others, reading the entire book can help you develop friendship skills even more effectively. The index can help you find information on topics of special interest to you.

As you read this book you'll notice quotes by youth. These youth are real, live human beings from several churches who responded to a survey on friendship.

You'll also notice **Read On** and **Stop and Think. Read On** encourages you to read a related section in the Bible or in this book. **Stop and Think** challenges you to explore your own thoughts and experiences to discover truth.

All good friendships take work. No friendship is easy or perfect. Even the closest friends fight, disagree, and struggle to understand each other. But all good friendships contain pleasure, promise, encouragement, and fulfillment. Learning how to deal with the problems can increase your friendship pleasures. This result is well worth the work!

Is building a friendship enjoyable? *Usually.*

Fulfilling? *Often.*

Easy? *Seldom.*

Worth it? *Always!*

"Be concerned for one another, to help one another to show love and to do good" (Heb. 10:24).

1
The Beginning: First Steps Toward Friendship

Norma is so happy. She has friends, confidence, and success. Norma and her friends never get into arguments. Her friends understand her and she understands them. Norma starts conversation with new people effortlessly. She continually makes new friends while keeping up with her current ones. Things run so smoothly for Norma.

But my life is a mess. I feel shy about meeting new people. Even after I manage to work up confidence I struggle to hide my nervousness. My friends and I get into fights. We misunderstand and disappoint each other. I get jealous and angry so easily. Why do I have so many problems? Why can't I be relaxed and get along with my friends like Norma? What's wrong with me?

Absolutely nothing.

Everyone everywhere, even Norma, struggles with making and keeping friends. Every friendship has both pleasures and problems. Norma works toward building friendships. She has friendship problems, but she and her friends talk them out. She wasn't born with confidence, calmness, and conversation skills. She gained them through practice.

Friendship is a skill. It takes skill to meet and get to know someone, to solve disagreements and problems, to understand and communicate. The goal of this book is to teach you these skills and to guide you toward understanding friendship truths. Equipped in this way, you can increase your friendship joys and conquer your friendship problems.

Getting Started

Whether you are in a new community, in a new school, with a new group, or with a new person, the task of making friends awaits you. What are the first steps? How do you handle your feelings of uneasiness?

"We're moving." The words hit with a thud. Lance's senior year was starting. He had been in the same town since kindergarten. Would he be accepted in the new school? Would he find friends as close as Greg and Steve? How would he meet people? Why couldn't he stay and finish high school in the same school like everybody else?

Dannielle had waited and waited; the time had finally come. She was entering the youth group at church. She was excited, but apprehensive. "How will I get to know the older youth group members? Will I fit in?"

Many might advise Lance and Dannielle to just "make friends." When asked how they make friends, youth said:

"I just do."

"I meet and get to know them."

"It just takes time."

"We talk about stuff like school and boys."

"I just meet people and if they like me and I like them, then we're friends."

But friendship doesn't always come this easily. There are specific actions that can help Lance and Danielle overcome their worries.

Here's How

Youth recommend these tips for making friends:

"Smile, say 'hi,' ask them something about class, eventually talk to them regularly, and hope!"

"Try to make the first move by starting a conversation or doing something with them."

"Invite them over to help with homework."

"Be open, introduce yourself. If you see a need, be there for them."

"Talk to them in school, ask them over, and watch your parent's reaction. Parents can often spot good friends."

"Share in their troubles. Comfort them. Spend time with them. Concentrating on their needs helps you worry less about your own nervousness."

Choose the Best

As you make friends, remember that you choose your friends. It does not just happen. You decide who to talk to and who to invite along. A high school senior said: "Choose your friends carefully. They are the ones who will help you with your problems and encourage your actions. Be certain to choose friends who will give good advice and encourage you to do and say the right things."

Who Shall I Choose as Friends?

When asked who they would choose as friends, people answered, "I choose friends . . .

. . . who approach me with a friendly attitude."

. . . who are Christians and who I can get along with."

. . . who accept me."

. . . who have actions I like."

. . . who can get along with anybody."

. . . who I can share with honestly and openly."

. . . who don't have to be in the 'in crowd.' "

. . . who strike me as really nice or needing a friend."

. . . who have the same interests I do."

. . . who have the same values I do."

. . . who are easy to talk to and the type person I am."

. . . who God would be proud of."

Hint: Your best friends will be the ones most like you. The saying "opposites attract" applies to magnets, not to relationships!

A Friendship Formula

It is almost always a little frightening to meet and get to know new people, but it can be fun with a little practice. Consider it an adventure. Try the following F.R.I.E.N.D.L.Y. formula. It explains the tips above.

"F" Is for First Move

Don't be afraid to make the first move. In your own nervousness you may forget that the other person may feel even more uncomfortable than you do. Concentrate on making your friend-to-be comfortable. Your warm smile and friendly hello will set your friend-to-be at ease.

Possible questions for starting a conversation with someone new are:

"What is your schedule this semester?"

"How do you like your classes so far?"

"What do you think of the cafeteria food?"

"Who is the best math teacher?"

"What do you like about your church?"

"What do you do in your spare time?"

Notice that many of these questions require more than a yes or no answer. The best friend-making questions promote conversation, not just one-word answers.

Don't expect or force things to happen all at once. The friend-making process is a gradual one. But the process must have a beginning. Let it be you!

"R" Is for Risk

Friend-making involves risk. When you make the first move, you risk being snubbed. But you also risk being accepted and genuinely liked. You'll never be liked without risking rejection. You must decide that the risk is worth it. Risk is scary; but without opening yourself up, you can never enjoy true friendship.

Becoming friends with someone unpopular brings another form of risk. Your current friends might reject you for choosing someone they have never liked well. On the other hand, you might discover a delightful friend and give your current friends the courage to get to know him.

No one had ever paid much attention to Lisa. Her teeth were crooked, and she didn't dress like everybody else. On a youth outing, Beth got stuck with her. As they talked, Beth discovered that Lisa could sing and play the guitar. The youth group needed musical talent! Beth invited Lisa to bring her guitar to the next meeting. Lisa sang beautifully, and she had a knack for helping others sing along. Beth wondered if anyone would have known about Lisa's ability if she had not gotten to know her.

"I" Is for Interest

As friendships develop, express genuine interest in your friends. What do they like to eat? Where do they like to go? What do they do after school? Who are their favorite people? Favorite songs? What irritates them? Makes them happy? How do they live their Christianity?

The subject people know most about is themselves. When you ask about their thoughts, dreams, and experiences and listen to what they share, your friends will love being around you. Your asking questions puts them at ease.

One way to show interest is to remember what friends tell

you. Ask about those topics the next time you talk. "Did you win the game?" "What were the test results?" "How are you feeling about her death?"

"E" is for Empathy

Empathy is a big word with an important meaning. It means to "feel with" someone you care about. An empathetic friend is sensitive to the moods, feelings, and thoughts of her friend. She understands. Empathy means to "Be happy with those who are happy, weep with those who weep" (Rom. 12:15).

Linda went to visit a friend whose mother had died the day before. When she returned home, her own mother asked: "What did you say?" Linda responded: "Nothing. I just sat down and cried with her."

That's empathy.

Sharing both happy and sad times with friends-to-be will draw you closer together.

"N" is for Being Needed

Being needed is a cozy feeling we all crave. Be sure to share with your friends the reasons you need them.

"I don't know what I'd do if I couldn't talk to you about this."

"I certainly needed your help with my homework last night! Thanks!"

"Nobody understands me like you do."

"D" Is for Being Dependable

The friends you develop will need you just as you will need them. Trust, which is essential to good friendships, cannot be earned if you are not dependable. Do you really keep the secrets your friend has told you? Will you support your friend at school when he is criticized or in a tight spot? Are you there when you say you'll be there?

"L" Is for Listening

Listen to your friends. Listening involves much more than using your ears. Your eyes listen by paying attention to another's expressions. Your head listens by nodding in understanding. Your hands listen by not doing something else when your friend is talking to you. Your body listens by turning toward your friend. Your mouth can listen by asking short questions or by saying, "I see what you mean!" Try using your whole self to hear what your friends are saying. You'll enjoy it, and they'll appreciate it.

"Y" Is for Being Yourself

Most important of all is being yourself.

Randall desperately wanted friends. He listened to people and studied their actions to learn just what they wanted in a friend. Around the cutups he cut up. Around the athletic types, he talked sports. Around the studious types, he compared grades. Soon, Randall had people around him all the time. But he still felt alone. He had no true friends because no one really knew him. They liked the image he had projected, not Randall. When Randall found the courage to be himself, he discovered that people liked him better than the image he had worked so hard to create.

Let your friends know the unique and special you.

Hint: Don't throw this formula away after your friendships begin. The same principles work toward keeping a friendship going!

Take It Slow

Of course you wouldn't try all of this the first week you meet someone. Consider Becca.

Becca craved friendship. She had moved to a new town for the fifth time in four years. She chose two people she liked, called each person daily, stayed with them at school; and asked them to do something with her at least twice a week. Soon they began to avoid her.

S-L-O-W is a key work for building friendships. No plant grows to maturity overnight. Neither do friendships. My wise grandfather said, "Things take time." As Becca discovered the hard way, it is unwise to try to build a friendship all at once. Instead, work at it steadily.

This principle also applies to conversation. Friends start by talking about the weather, school events, and mutual interests. They gradually progress to sharing dreams, hopes, worries, and secrets. Build trust and gain one another's confidence before delving into issues like:

"Who do you like?"

"My problem is. . . . What do you think I should do?"

"How do you know God is real?"

"How do you get along with your parents so well?"

Cultivate Your Friendship

Think of friendship as a garden. Beginning a friendship is similar to planting the seeds. To keep your friendship healthy you must take good care of it. Weed out the negatives by recognizing them when they occur, talking about them, and refusing to let them continue. Cultivate the positives by practicing them and by substituting them when a negative threatens to occur.

Cultivate:

- understanding
- cooperation
- listening
- acceptance
- communication
- support
- openness
- sensitivity
- respect

Weed Out:

- selfishness
- insecurity
- deception
- bitterness
- fear
- betrayal
- anger
- jealousy
- gossip

2
Me: If I Don't Like Myself, Nobody Will

A Feeling About Me

The single most important factor in finding and enjoying friends is how you feel about yourself. The Bible says to love others as we love ourselves (Matt. 22:39) and to love as Jesus loves us (John 15:12).

But God blew it when He created me. He may like me, but He's the only one. I trip walking up to make a report. I say the wrong thing at the wrong time. I get the giggles during important discussions. Who would like someone who does these things? I certainly don't. If I can't like myself, who will?

That's exactly the point. Jesus knew what He was talking about. If we do not care for ourselves, we cannot build healthy friendships. People notice how we feel about ourselves and tend to believe us.

A person who believes she is likable is free to

- like others;
- to both succeed and fail;
- to admit both accomplishments and failures.

A person who believes he is worth something
will choose friends and dates who treat him well.

A person confident of God's love
will have the courage to live Christianity.

But, a person who does not feel likable
will be so preoccupied with trying to be liked
that he will not be able to care about his friends.
A person who does not value herself
will put up with people who treat her rotten,
thinking she can get no better treatment.
A person who is insecure
will insist that he does no wrong and
may be threatened by a friend's accomplishments.
A person who fears that God doesn't like her
will hesitate to live her Christianity.

Stop and Think: "Putting yourself down is as bad as being conceited. Either way, you're focusing on yourself." How is this statement accurate?

Find Someone to Coach You

Dody was convinced that everyone hated her. She was too tall, wore braces, and maintained a face full of pimples. She knew no one would want to talk to such an ugly specimen of humanity. She didn't say much and avoided situations where she would have to meet people. Her mother called her fears silly but her aunt listened to her worries. She suggested that Dody say "hi" to one new person the next day. Dody agreed, but didn't think she could do it.

The next morning she was uneasy about talking to someone new. But feeling worse about letting her aunt down, she hurriedly said "hi" to someone on her way into homeroom. She slid into her seat relieved and proud of herself.

Her aunt's words of praise were worth it all.

Gradually Dody's aunt prescribed harder friend-making tasks. Over the next several months, Dody's confidence soared. Fifteen years later, her self-esteem still takes an occasional nosedive, but she is growing.

Dody's aunt taught her three important principles about learning to like herself:

Take it slow. You won't overcome negative feelings about yourself in one day. Friendship fears take time to conquer. Your negative feelings about yourself took a long time developing. They'll take a long time to change.

It's hard, but worth it. Learning to become outgoing is hard at first. It becomes easier as you succeed in little ways. The new friends are worth the work, uneasiness, and worry.

A supportive friend helps. Dody's aunt believed in her and encouraged her to develop her friend-making skills. She coached her gently and with support. An adult friend or a mature peer can do the same for you.

Concentrate on Other People

We forget that other people worry about being liked, too. Many of the people you want to be friends with are worrying about whether you like them. If you concentrate on making them comfortable, you will find yourself forgetting all about your own fears. You'll find you've made friends simply by making their needs more important than your own.

To keep from dwelling on yourself, concentrate on these tasks:

Look for the Good Qualities in Your Friends

Tell them what you see. Does Judy have gorgeous eyes? Say so! Can Dan help you solve your problems by the way he listens to you? Thank him! Did Rachel succeed at a difficult activity? Congratulate her!

Most of us have a hard time seeing our good points. Pointing out the good in others is called "affirmation." Affirmation brings out the best in people and is a powerful friendship builder.

Be Sensitive to Problems

Did someone hint that things were just awful yesterday? *Tell me about it* is a good way to show that you are interested in the friend's problem. Your listening ear and your concern make your friend's problem seem smaller. They will cherish your friendship and will likely be there when you need help.

Include Others

Look for people who are standing by themselves or who are not with the rest of the crowd. They crave being involved and accepted. Talk with them. Invite them to sit with you or to join you in conversation. You'll gain a new friend and they'll feel at home.

Risk Sharing Yourself

No friendship develops without risk. To be liked, you must risk being rejected. Most people will like you more when you be yourself. The ones that don't aren't much fun. Genuineness and honesty are top-rated friendship qualities. They're worth the risk.

Tell your friends when something good happens or when something frustrating strikes. Give others the opportunity to be excited for you and the chance to share your sadness, or help you with your problem. A big part of making friends is sharing yourself.

Hint: Discover you can trust a person before you share important thoughts and dreams. Not everyone keeps secrets or handles thoughts sensitively. Seek those who can.

Talk Until You Understand

Talking and working toward understanding are essential to feeling good about yourself. You might think every problem is your fault. But problems have many causes. Understanding the actual reasons enables you to attack the problem, not yourself.

Amy couldn't understand why Janie was so obsessed with making good grades. Amy repeatedly became irritated with Janie because Janie so often studied when Amy wanted to do something. Amy decided to talk with Janie about it when she wasn't feeling irritated.

"Why do you study all the time?" Amy asked. "It makes me feel like you don't like me or something!"

"Oh no! It's definitely not that I don't like you! I love spending time with you," Janie quickly responded. "I want to be a pharmacist. The school I want to attend requires a high grade-point average. Because it's really important to me to get into that school, I want to do all I can to get accepted!"

Amy sighed with relief, "That certainly makes me feel better! Maybe we could study together the next time I want to get together and you have plans to study."

This simple conversation saved Amy and Janie much pain, frustration, worry, and anger. It took courage for Amy to lay out her feelings. It took sensitivity and openness on both sides to express, understand, and accept the other's feelings. Janie showed her friendship by reassuring Amy of her care. Amy showed her friendship by being willing to alter her plans to study with Janie.

Spend Time with Friends

Melinda's fear of rejection often keeps her from going to church activities, parties, ball games, school functions, and other group events. She gets so nervous ahead of time, that she doesn't feel it's worth going.

The only way Melinda will become comfortable around others is to be with them. Because friend making is a skill and skills require practice, Melinda must "practice" being with groups. After forcing herself to go a few times, she will begin to feel at home.

As you make friends, spend time with them. Participate in a variety of activities. The more friends talk, the more places they go, and the more different experiences they share, the closer they become. The closer you feel to your friend, the less you will worry if she likes you.

Read On: The "Sweethearts" chapter includes a long list of activities friends can do together.

Choose Positive Friends

Develop a positive view of yourself by exposing yourself to people who like themselves. Their comfort will help you be comfortable. Talk to these people when you have a problem. They will guide you to attack it from the right perspective.

The people we choose to be with guide us toward becoming the people we are. Choose friends whom you want to be like. Choose friends who bring out the good in you, who affirm your strengths, who accept your weaknesses.

That sounds really great, but where do I find these people and experiences?

Seek them out wherever you go: school, part-time jobs, church, sports events, camp, retreats, Bible studies, service opportunities, and more.

In any situation, you meet both positive and negative people, constructive and destructive activities. Consider the following as you decide which are which:

- Are you comfortable around this person?
- Does this person make you feel free to live and talk about Christianity?
- Does this person help you feel good about yourself?
- Would you want Jesus to watch what you are doing?

• Does this person encourage your strengths and tolerate your weaknesses?

The more "yes" answers, the more likely the friend will help develop a more likable you.

But my friends are already chosen! The only way to start over is to move to another town or school and that's not an option for me. What do I do about friends who are destructive to me?

Limit your contact with those who encourage you to compromise your values or who bring you down. The easiest way to do this is to be busy with positive friends and activities. Discover a few friends and experiences which increase your enjoyment of yourself and of life. Build from there until most of your friends bring out the best in you. By then, you may have the strength to bring out the best in others!

Read On: "Popularity" addresses this question, too.

There are still times . . .

I believe all this about loving myself before I can be a good friend. But there are still certain people who make me feel awkward or incompetent.

Sonya is one of those super attractive and popular girls who makes guys forget about the importance of personality. Even the other girls want to be like her. I feel awkward and ugly when she's around.

Inside I know that she is an unhappy person, that her family has troubles, and that she struggles to get good grades. But nobody really cares about that. Because she is rich and attractive, people like her. My close family, ability to make friends, and good grades seem worthless when she's around.

Does this kind of person intimidate you? If not, substitute one who does as you work through these steps.

1. *Recognize it.* To conquer this problem you must first real-

ize that you are uncomfortable when certain people are around.

2. *Understand it.* What is it about this person that makes you uncomfortable? Is she prettier or richer than you? Does she say or do things that irritate you? Has this person hurt you in the past? Does she criticize you or others?

3. *Accept it.* It is normal to feel uncomfortable around certain persons. Your discomfort has nothing to do with your value or worth. Accept that even though you don't *feel* lovable, you are lovable.

4. *Act on reality.* God has instructed us to love everyone, but this doesn't mean we will like them all. We do not have to be close to every person. We do need to treat them considerately and as worthwhile persons.

5. *Get a good dose of people you do feel comfortable around.* Their friendships can give you the confidence you need to handle situations in which you don't feel loved or appreciated.

P. S. An interesting twist to the uncomfortable relationship problem is that the people you feel rejected by may also be worrying about being accepted. This makes it worth concentrating on accepting rather than being accepted.

3
Disappointments: Oh, No! What Now?

What do you do when your friends let you down?

- Give up on them?
- Decide they must not have been true friends after all?
- Vow to let them down next time?

Though natural reactions, none of these are satisfactory solutions. They are based on the myth: "True friends never disappoint each other." In real life, even the closest friends disappoint and fail one another occasionally.

Poor communication
not realizing the other's needs,
seeing only our side of the situation,
fears,
irritabilities,
bad moods,
differing expectations
are some of the reasons friends hurt one another. We need to accept these not as God's perfect plan for friendship but as part of our human shortcomings.

It Happened to Jesus

Peter, who loved Jesus dearly, denied Him three times (Matt. 26:69-75). This problem caused incredible pain but it did not destroy their relationship. The problem was solved and the relationship continued.

Just as Jesus dealt with the problem and then continued to love and relate to Peter, we can solve our friendship disappointments by dealing with the problem and then continuing to love and relate to each other. Our steady loving can bring out the best in each other and may make disappointments less frequent.

There Is an Answer

What do you do when your friends let you down? That's a big question. And a hard question. But it has answers. The answer is not simple like the answer to, "What do you do when the light turns red?" Its a more complicated answer like one which answers, "How do you win a football game?"

In a ball game, as in friendship, no one thing ensures a win. Instead, several factors working together result in victory. Healing a broken friendship is the product of many actions and attitudes.

You Win Some, You Lose Some, and Some Are Rained Out

In both football and friendship you're going to win some, lose some, and some will be rained out. Some problems can be solved easily. Others may be hard to solve or may not be solved. Some you may never have the opportunity to solve.

In football, winning against the big rival is more impressive than against a team that is not known as well. A lot more energy goes into the first win. Likewise, it makes a big difference whether the one who disappoints you is your see-only-at-school friend or your calls-you-every-night-and-with-whom-you-share-every-secret-problem-and-dream friend. It's the difference between being grounded for one day of the week and being grounded every day of the week. The principles in both are the same, but the second instance affects life more deeply.

It's All in the Approach

The way the other team is approached is as important as who it is. Being up for the game and hitting the other team head-on are effective in football. These approaches work with friends too.

Suppose your calls-you-every-night-and-with-whom-you-share-your-every-secret-problem-and-dream friend hurts you. You told her who you like after she promised never to tell anyone. But you just found out that she told *him*! (Boys, substitute a similar situation.) How could she have done this to you? What will you do now?

You have three options.

One: You could stop being her friend. After all, anyone who would betray someone like this can't be much of a friend!

The only problem with this solution is that eventually you will run out of friends. Because none of us has achieved the ability to live perfectly, we all let each other down sooner or later.

Two: You could talk about it. After all, you two have had plenty of experience talking. But you've never talked about anything this hard. You're not sure how to do it.

Three: Maybe it would be better to just not talk about it. Forget it. After all, that is easier; and it hurts much less.

The third solution may be easier, but it certainly won't hurt less. Your own sad and angry feelings which you keep inside will eat away at you rather than be forgotten. They will dominate your thoughts and take away your appetite. Perhaps, worst of all, they will eat at your friendship because you won't feel like being around your friend.

Talk It Out

Well, OK, if it's better to talk about it and meet the broken friendship head-on, what do I say?

How you play and what you say depends a great deal on your coach. A coach who is out to win the game at any cost will advise differently than one who wants to play hard but fair.

In mending broken friendships we can choose ourselves for a coach. Some of us coach by "get even so she won't take advantage of me anymore!" Others coach by "don't rock the boat or my friend won't like me anymore." Neither of these heals friendship pain very effectively.

A more effective coach is Jesus. He can make us secure enough to do deal with the problem directly and constructively. He would encourage us to do all we can to mend the friendship. What does the Bible suggest saying?

> Do not use harmful words, but only helpful words, the kind that build up and provide what is needed, so that what you say will do good to those who hear you (Eph. 4:29).

When mending a friendship, put your feelings and thoughts into honest but caring words. You may feel like punching your friend, but tame it a bit and say something like "I am really angry and hurt that you told Chuck that I like him! I don't understand why you did that! Would you explain?"

Of course, this type of conversation takes more than a passing moment in the hall. Ask your friend for some time to discuss something important. Find a place where you can talk without interruption.

When the time comes, you will probably feel nervous and uneasy. It's good to say so directly: "This is hard for me to talk about. I am really nervous. Please hear what I am trying to say because the words might not come out just right. I am not trying to hurt you but to help our friendship. I want to attack a problem, not you."

The conversation will probably make your friend just as nervous as you are. She may also be a bit defensive. Listen to your friend's responses with care and sensitivity, trying to put her at ease.

"But she's the one who hurt me! Why should I be the one to put her at ease?" you think.

If she is at ease, there is a better chance of solving the problem. If you provoke your friend, her anger will increase, which will increase your anger, which will increase hers, and so on. Your problems will multiply, not be conquered. Getting to the root of the problem, not planting more seeds of conflict is your goal.

You may ask "Why do I have to start the process if she is the one who did wrong? Shouldn't I wait for her to apologize?"

Jesus advised in Matthew 5:23-24 and 18:15 that we are to go to the person who wrongs us rather than wait for her to come to us. This is very hard and seems backward, but it has a peculiar catch: It works!

Perhaps the friend doesn't realize what she has done. Maybe she doesn't know how much she has hurt you. Even if she does know, holding anger in eats away at you. God knows that getting the hurt and angry feelings out benefits you as well as your friends.

What Caused the Problem?

As you continue the conversation with the "Coach" guiding you, listen for why the problem happened.

- Did she forget that you had asked her not to tell?
- Did Chuck ask her if you liked him?
- Was she trying to get you together with him?
- Was she jealous and wanted the fellow for herself?

What she says may make you feel better or it may make you even more angry. Tell her how you feel by saying something like: "That definitely makes more sense. I was really confused and hurt. I understand better now." (or) "I really am hurt that you did this. Maybe you did not know it would hurt me so much. I need your apology."

It Takes Two

No matter how well one team plays, the actions and attitudes of the other team influence the outcome of the game. The other team may play a good, fair game, attacking the ball and not the players; or they may hurt the best players in order to win.

In friendship mending, your friend may accept your words and attempts to solve the problem. She may join with you to attack the problem. Or she may attack you with words such as, "You aren't much of a friend to become so angry with me! If you really liked me, you wouldn't accuse me of such things!"

You cannot be responsible for your friend's responses, but you must be responsible for your own. Resist becoming defensive in return. You can say, "It is because I am your friend that I come to you. Let's attack the problem and not each other."

Caring is usually contagious. But if it is not, continue your responsiblity to "do everything possible . . . to live in peace with everybody" (Rom. 12:18).

Forgive, and Move On

Before the end of the game, it is helpful to call a time-out to decide the final play. Part of the final play in friendship mending must be forgiveness.

Forgiveness is never easy, but without it there remain blocks in your relationship with God (Matt. 6:14-15) and your relationship with your friend. Remember that forgiveness does not mean you have to forget. It does mean that you get rid of bitter feelings and that you reaffirm your acceptance of your friend.

Just as a successful block prevents a good play, failing to forgive keeps anger and hurt right in the middle of friendship. This prevents closeness from developing.

Forgive your friend and tell her so. You might say: "I still don't feel really good about this, but I do forgive you. My feelings will follow." (or) "I am feeling better about this. I forgive you. Thanks for working on this with me."

Read On: Matthew 6:14-15 explains that failing to forgive others can block our relationship with God. Why do you think this is true?

What Next?

Make decisions about how to continue the relationship. You may want to remind your friend not to tell your secrets. You may want to decide you can no longer tell her important secrets. (It is not necessary to tell her this.) You can still be friends, but not tell every secret, wish, and dream so freely.

There are times when changing the closeness of a friendship is good. It might change because of different values ("to tell or not to tell") or when interests change. This is normal and natural. The important factor is that the changes occur in the loving way of Jesus. Whether it is continuing the friendship at the same level, becoming closer, or becoming less close, both of you can know the next play.

Read On: Chapter 10, "The End," contains more detail on changing friendships.

Shake Hands

Finally, no matter who wins the football game, it is important to shake hands and congratulate the winner. After the friendship-mending conversation, shake hands symbolically by reaffirming and renewing the friendship. Say such important words as: "I'm sorry this had to happen, but I'm glad we've talked it out." and "I'm glad you're my friend."

When your friends let you down from time to time, you and they are normal! It still hurts when friends disappoint you, but take steps to heal the hurt and to help it happen less often.

There is one principle which is not possible in football, but almost always happens in friendship mending—both sides can win!

Read On: The Bible says in Romans 12:18; Mark 9:50; and 1 Peter 3:11 to do everything possible to live at peace with your friends. How do the principles in this chapter enable you to have peaceful friendships?

4
Conflicts: Fight the Problem, Not the Person

Angie and Julia fought often. Angie became angry any time Julia's opinion differed from hers. Angie thought friends should always agree. Julia felt friends should be themselves even when their opinions differed.

When Angie talked with other girls, Julia became jealous and said that Angie didn't really like her. Julia wanted Angie to be her best and only friend. Angie wanted to be best friends, but felt she could have other friends, too.

Matt and Sharon enjoyed each other. Sharon understood Matt's dating problems and parent problems. Matt was able to help Sharon see things from another point of view. Matt thought Sharon was a little impulsive, but he liked her anyway. Sharon thought Matt took things too seriously, but that was OK. Matt and Sharon knew they could be themselves around each other and they would be accepted. They could talk about almost anything and feel comfortable.

Who Are the Friends?

These two relationships are quite different.

Matt and Sharon	**Julia and Angie**
work out their differences;	fight out their differences;
have a calm friendship;	have a stormy friendship;
accept one another;	frustrate each other;

enjoy their friendship; are miserable together;
understand each other. misunderstand each other.

Which ones are friends? Both. Despite all the differences there are basic similarities.

All four persons are
sincerely trying to build good friendships;
need friends;
really care about each other
have conflict.

Conquer Conflict

Every friendship has conflicts. Whenever there is more than one person, there is potential for differences of opinion. The conflict itself is not bad, but the way you deal with it can be. The differences must be worked out.

Because Matt and Sharon talked out their differences, their relationship was enjoyable. Julia and Angie's conflicts overwhelmed them. Why?

Matt and Sharon learned how to conquer conflict. It did not come naturally. This friendship skill came through:

- Good friendships
- Parents
- Relatives
- Books
- Bible studies
- Television and movies
- Teachers
- Youth workers
- Children
- Classes

Unfortunately the same places Matt and Sharon learned their positive problem-solving skills were the places Angie and Julia learned negative problem-solving skills. Matt and Sharon were lucky enough to have had positive people and experiences.

But it doesn't have to be luck. You can choose to grow positive problem-solving skills by choosing positive people and experiences. Notice who you spend time with. Pay attention to the shows you watch and the experiences you participate in. It's up to you to choose the best. Your friendships are affected by every person and experience you encounter. Be certain the influence is a good one.

Cultivate the Positives

Positive problem-solving methods encourage solutions. They attack the problem, not the person. Negative methods are destructive. They attack the person, not the problem. They cause more problems than they solve.

Practice these positive problem-solving methods:

- trust
- honesty
- acceptance
- faithfulness
- give and take
- Christian commitment
- communication
- sensitivity
- listening
- respect
- care and kindness
- availability
- support.

When you notice destructive methods in yourself, replace them with postive ones. Then talk about those destructive urges with someone you trust and pray about them until you no longer have the desire to use them.

Some of these destructive characteristics are:

- dishonesty
- moodiness
- cruel words
- keeping things inside
- failure to communicate
- not taking time for each other
- jealousy of time spent with others

- jealousy of looks, clothes, position
- trying to be something you're not
- failing to be there when a friend needs you
- pressuring the other to deny his convictions.

Fighting Fair

The dilemma between Angie and Julia was not that they fought, but that they did not fight fair. All friends have conflicts and problems. There are ways to express these disagreements that improve rather than destroy friendship.

A communications specialist has called this "fighting fair." You can remember how to fight fair through Wade Rowatt's rhyming formula: name, claim, aim, and flame/tame.

Name the problem. Get it out in the open and define it so that both sides are comfortable.

Claim your part of it. Instead of accusing the other, look at your contribution to the problem. Most problems have two contributors. Saying "I" more than "you" can keep you from accusing unfairly.

Aim your anger and frustration at the problem, not at your friend. Fight the problem, not the person.

Flame your part of the discussion if you fear talking about problems. This does not mean to burn, but to gently become more open with your thoughts and feelings.

Tame your words and emotions if you lose your temper, say cruel things, or yell.

Need a Referee? When you and your friend have trouble talking out your disagreements, you may need a referee. Such a person can help you solve your problem by guiding you to discuss your feelings and thoughts in a constructive way. Choose a trusted adult such as a parent, minister, or teacher.

Destructive Fighting

Think about the way you solve disagreements with your friends. Are you guilty of any of these "dirty fighting" techniques?

1. "I don't want to talk about it!" (Making a friend feel bad by refusing to talk to him.)

2. "Julia, you never do what I want! I don't think that's right do you, Sandy?" (Taking a shot at the friend in public so others will think she's horrible.)

3. "That Angie is always mad about something!" (Gossip or talking behind backs.)

4. "You're just mad because Jeb broke up with you!" (Bringing up old "sore spots.")

5. "If you go without me I'll never be your friend again." (Winning by force or threat.)

Attack the Problem, Not Each Other

Try this more effective way of solving problems. It can be more difficult, but it works. The "dirty fighting" techniques are easy but destroy friendships.

1. Identify and define the problem.

What can Julia and Angie agree on? Julia might define one of their problems by saying, "Angie, I would like to be able to express my opinion without you becoming angry. When I disagree, I still like you."

Angie might define it, "Julia, I want you to agree with me so that I know you understand me."

A mutual definition might be, "Disagreeing bothers us and we need a better way to deal with it."

2. List every possible solution.

Together the girls could write a list. Listing every solution that comes to mind, even those they might not try, assures that they talk without judging each other's ideas.

The list might include:

A. Just don't mention it when we disagree.

B. Assure each other that we care even when we disagree.

C. Quit being friends because of our disagreements.

D. Prove who is right.

E. Agree to disagree.

F. Talk until we understand each other's point of view even when disagreeing.

3. Evaluate the possiblities.

Neither girl is ready to quit being friends, so they eliminate solution C. Solution A would create frustration for Julia so she crossed out that one. Solution D would create even more fighting because both might have valid opinions.

Both girls like options B, E, and F.

4. Choose the best solution.

More talking convinced both Julia and Angie that F was the best solution. If they understood each other, Angie would likely feel assured of Julia's care and Julia would feel free to be herself.

5. Put the solution into practice.

Julia tried to convince Angie that their solution would take hard work. She vowed to assure Angie of her care before she told her a differing opinion. Angie agreed to count to ten before reacting to a difference or problem. She thought this might help her get a handle on her anger. Both agreed to restate what the other was saying to be certain they understood.

6. Follow up to evaluate how the solution worked.

This severe problem will take a long time to work out. Angie will probably lose her temper several times while learning to control it. Julia will likely forget to reassure Angie. But the two agree to talk again in a month to check their progress and to encourage each other.

Check Your Emotions

Unharnessed emotion can destroy even the best attempts at problem solving. Anger is the most dangerous. Anger is not bad, but the ways we express it can become destructive. We can use it to attack, control, criticize, belittle, or win. Talking about anger can prevent its destructiveness and insure that both sides win.

Anger can mean many things:

- I'm afraid.
- I'm hurt.
- I'm confused.
- I feel helpless.
- I feel attacked.
- I feel used.
- I have too much to do.
- I'm tired.
- I think you don't like me.
- I'm angry.

Notice anger in yourself. Talk about it. Search for the reasons behind it.

I'm feeling really angry. I think it's because I feel taken advantage of. I don't think you mean to do that. Can we talk about it?

When your friend becomes angry, try to respond calmly. Together, search for the reasons. Realize that you are not always the reason for that anger.

"You seem really mad!" said Madelyn.

"You bet I am! I can't believe he did that to you!" responded Nate.

"Oh, I thought you were mad at me!" said Madelyn, relieved.

"No, I just hate to see you hurt this way." said Nate.

Concentrate on Meeting Needs

Some conflicts come when friends ignore the other's needs. Worry, disappointment, fatigue, and frustration sometimes make friends fight. Such fights can be prevented by a little listening, comforting, and understanding.

Notice why your friend is grouchy. Did he stay up all night studying? Did her mom yell at her? Rather than another fight, your friend needs some extra concern.

Many days Matt is frustrated and tired. He has little to give. On those days, Sharon gives more than she receives. Other days, Sharon is the one with needs. She feels useless and ugly. She needs for Matt to point out the good in her. She needs to be reminded of the good she does.

If you are the grouchy one, communicate that to your friend. This warns your friend to be sensitive and helps your friend know what you need.

Denise, I've had a horrible morning. If I snap at you, it's nothing personal. I'm just feeling tired and irritable. Please bear with me.

Alan, I need to complain to somebody. You don't need to say anything. In fact I might get irritated if you do. I just want to spout off. Then I'll feel better.

When your friend is unhappy, ignore your own needs and do most of the giving. That's OK. Because next time you'll be on the receiving end.

It is crucial that each friend do some of the giving and some of the receiving. If you always do all the giving or all the receiving, something is wrong. Try to balance it.

"And look out for one another's interests, not just for your own. The attitude you should have is the one that Christ Jesus had" (Phil. 2:4-5).

Notice Your Influence

Conflicts can be eased by concentrating on the way you affect your friends. Thinking ahead about what you say and do can prevent much pain. The conflicts caused by our own thoughtless words and actions much easier to prevent than to "fix" later. Your words and actions make a difference.

Friends Can

help us handle our problems	*or*	make us feel more discouraged.
work out problems with us	*or*	attack us.
help us like ourselves	*or*	make us hate ourselves.
motivate us to accept others	*or*	encourage us to snub them.
help us live Christianity	*or*	keep us from Christianity.

Notice your words and actions. Choose those that influence your friends positively, as in the left column. Find friends who do the same for you.

Read On: Matthew 18:15-17 gives guidelines for solving problems between friends.

Chapter 5, "Communication," gives tips on how to choose words and actions.

5
Communication: Feeling Understood

He never understands me! Even when we disagree, I need to communicate my ideas and know that he understands why I feel and think as I do. Even if my fears are silly to him, I want him to understand why I'm afraid. When we have different plans, I want to talk about them until we can agree on a plan that pleases us both.

Communication. They say it's the most important factor in the success of a relationship. Why is it so hard?

Any time there is more than one person, there is potential for more than one opinion, emotion, and plan. Through talking, hearing, and understanding, two people communicate these opinions, emotions, and plans.

Communication takes know-how, patience, love, and work. This chapter provides some of the know-how. You add the willingness to work, the patience, and the love. Then enjoy the closer friendship that results!

What Is Communication?

Communication occurs when what is in your head and heart matches what is in my head and heart. It does not mean we agree but we understand the other's thoughts and feelings. Understanding says, "What you say and do and think is worthwhile. It makes sense."

To say what we want to say, we must train our words, our actions, and our attitudes.

Communication is not:	*Communication is:*
• always agreeing	• hearing
• always accepting	• understanding
• saying anything you want	• harnessing emotions
• easy	• trying to feel as the other feels
• over in one try	• talking until both friends are comfortable
• one-sided	• two-sided

Communication Myths

Believing and acting on communication myths can destroy your friendship. Which of these three myths is most likely to invade your friendship?

Myth # 1: *"True friends never disagree."* No two people agree on everything. Disagreements arise in any relationship, but they do not have to be destructive. True friends know how to handle their disagreements without negative emotions.

When disagreements arise, talk about them until each understands the other's point of view. Arrive at a mutual solution.

Myth # 2: *"If friends really love each other, communication will come naturally."* Communication is a learned skill. Some people have simply learned their lessons better than others. Read and practice. Like all skills, communication improves with practice.

Myth # 3: *"She should know how I feel without my having to tell her."* Nobody can read minds. No friendship outgrows the need to talk. Even couples who have been married fifty years must talk, share feelings, and work to understand each other better.

This myth arose because it is possible to notice moods and emotions without talking. However:

Quiet might mean	Noise might mean:
"I'm sad."	"I'm excited."
"I'm sick."	"I'm nervous."
"I'm mad."	"I'm embarrassed."
"I'm sleepy."	"I'm angry."
"I'm shy."	"I'm happy."
"I think you don't care."	"I'm afraid you won't."

How do you find out which is meant? Talk, using some of the methods described in this chapter: ask questions, use your whole body to communicate, listen, accept what is said, and show concern.

When Susan and her boyfriend fight, Susan becomes depressed. So when Diedre noticed Susan looking sad, she assumed it was boyfriend problems again:

"You must have had another fight with Jason. Come on, let's get a soda," encouraged Diedre.

"No, Jason and I are fine. Why do you ask?" said Susan.

"You're so sad looking," responded Diedre.

"Oh, that! I just stayed up late studying for an algebra test and I'm exhausted." said Susan.

Diedre had to talk with Susan to discover the true reason for her sadness. Diedre could notice sadness without words but she wrongly assessed the reason for the sadness without talking.

Choose Your Words Carefully

Choosing the right words and saying them the right way is crucial to communication. Ephesians 4:29 reminds us to "not use harmful words, but only helpful words, the kind that build up and provide what is needed, so that what you say will do good to those who hear you."

Harmful Words Produce:	Helpful Words Produce:
sarcasm	encouragement
ridicule	reassurance

shaming	affirmation
cruelty	kindness
boastfulness	understanding

James explained that the words we choose demonstrate the beliefs we hold: "Does anyone think he is religious? If he does not control his tongue, his religion is worthless and he deceives himself" (Jas. 1:26).

How do we follow James's advice? Ask yourself, "What would God think of these words?" Choose words that encourage communication. Reject those that inhibit it.

The timing of your words is as important as the words you choose.

Encourage Communication

Add encouraging attitudes and a tone of voice that shoes love and understanding.

Encouraging Words		Inhibiting Words
I feel	*rather than*	You did it
Please	*rather than*	You have to
I'm concerned	*rather than*	I'm disgusted with you
I'm hurt	*rather than*	You hurt me again
Can we work on it?	*rather than*	You'd better change
I understand	*rather than*	That's a dumb feeling
I'll work on it	*rather than*	How dare you accuse me?
I don't agree	*rather than*	You're wrong

Encouraging Attitudes	Inhibiting Attitudes
Understanding	Accusation
Concern	Defensiveness
Respect	Anger
Gentleness	Agressiveness
Vulnerablity	Low self-concept

Find the communication encouragers and inhibitors in these

three conversations. How would you change the words to improve communication?

Bud: We're both working towards valedictorian. I fear our competing against each other is becoming more important than our concern for each other.

Paul: You're just saying that to get me to back off. It's just an underhanded way to insure your winning!

Bud encouraged communication by telling how he felt rather than accusing. He also included himself in the problem. But, Paul inhibited communication by accusing Bud. A more receptive response might be: "You may be right. But I still want to have the highest grades. What can we do about it?" This would keep the two boys talking instead of building a wall between them. They could then attack the problem instead of each other.

Takkia: Marie, if you don't quit drinking so much you're going to become an alcoholic!

Marie: That's easy for you to say. You don't know what my situation is like!

Takkia is concerned about Marie's drinking. But her concern came across as judgment. This inhibited communication by causing Marie to become defensive. A better start might be: "Marie, I'm really concerned about you. You get sad and then drink. Would you like to talk about what's bothering you?"

Jay: Peter, I'm concerned about something. When we're around certain people, I feel that you ignore me.

Peter: I don't mean to. You are an important friend to me. When I'm around the popular people, I become so preoccupied with impressing them that I ignore you. I'm sorry. It's not deliberate.

Jay wanted to tell Peter how much it hurts to be ignored. He encouraged communication by gently sharing how he felt. Peter encouraged communication by understanding, by reassuring Jay of his care for him, and by admitting accidental wrong. It took much pride swallowing by both boys to share so openly and sensitively. Because they were willing to do this, their friendship improved.

Hint: Even if your friend uses communication inhibitors, you can encourage communication. Your eagerness to talk openly can be contagious. Reread the list of encouragers.

More Than Your Mouth

Becky was ecstatic! She flung the door open with excitement. "Mom, he likes me! I can tell by the way he looks at me!"

Josh was frustrated. "I just cannot get my teacher to notice me. In class he calls me 'You, in the third row.' In the halls he ignores me. Why doesn't he like me?"

Becky's boyfriend did not say he liked her, nor did Josh's teacher say he did not like him. Each person made a decision based on the actions of another. Actions, as well as words, are crucial to communication.

To communicate you use your:

- eyes
- hands
- ears
- mouth
- tone of voice
- feet
- facial expression
- shoulders
- arms
- fingers
- head

Eyes can communicate love or scorn.
Ears can listen or simply decorate a head.
A voice can say "Mm hmmm" or can sigh with boredom.
A face can look interested or disgusted.
A head can nod with interest or turn away.
Arms can pull toward or push away.
Hands can caress or slap.

Fingers can show involvement or boredom.

Feet can walk with or avoid someone.

The first action in each pair says: "I'm interested in you!" or "I like you! The second action says, "Neither you nor what you say is important."

It may seem peculiar that a voice can listen. A voice listens by timing its words and by repeating what a friend says.

Timing: Count to ten silently before you speak. This ensures that you will not interrupt your friend. Also, consider how what you say affects your friend.

Repeating: State in your own words what you heard your friend say. *"You seem hurt that your dad didn't even notice your good grade. He commented only on the bad ones."* This gives your friend a chance to clarify any misunderstanding you have.

Show You Mean It

When a friend is talking, you show you are bored or disinterested when you:

- turn away.
- doodle as he talks to you.
- look at the floor.
- find yourself yawning.

You show interest and concern when you:

- turn toward her.
- look with interest at his face.
- nod as you listen to each word.
- smile.

Pay attention to what your words and body are saying. You may be communicating rejection without meaning to do so. You may be failing to show love to someone you care about. Just as you can control your tongue, you can control what your body says.

Accept Your Friend's Thoughts and Feelings

"Will you like me?" We worry that our friends will quit liking us if we feel or think differently than they do. We also fear that friends will think we don't like them if we express frustration with something they say or do. This makes honest communication difficult.

Acceptance frees us to communicate honestly with our friends.

Diane wanted Dan to give her roses every Valentine's Day. Dan preferred to bring Diane roses on a nonholiday. Diane had trouble accepting Dan's way of caring. She felt that not giving her roses on Valentine's Day meant that he did not care about her. Dan thought it artificial to give flowers on a prescribed day. He wanted to choose his own day.

How can Dan and Diane communicate openly and still share their differing feelings and thoughts? Their conversation might go like this:

"You seem sad Diane. Is something bothering you?" asked Dan.

"Well, yes. It's Valentines Day and you didn't even remember." responded Diane.

"You know I have trouble with dates," confessed Dan "And besides, I don't like for anyone to tell me when to give you roses. I want to think of it myself. If a day tells me to do it, my giving doesn't seem sincere."

"I guess that makes sense," admitted Diane. "And you did bring me a rose last month for no reason."

"Sure there was a reason! I love you!" grinned Dan.

"I love you, too. Thanks for helping me understand," said Diane, relieved.

By honestly expressing their views and feelings, this couple understood each other, and could more easily accept one another. It took courage for Diane to share her feelings without accusing. Dan showed concern by not becoming defensive and reassuring Diane of his love.

Talk about your differences. All friends have them.

If you can resolve the differences, marvelous.

If you can accept them ("agree to disagree"), good.

If they divide you permanently, move on.

If you cannot talk about differences, it's a sign that your friendship is not healthy.

Practice, Practice, and Practice Some More

Communication is a skill that grows with practice. Practice communicating with everyone you know. Rehearse in your head what you will say and what they might say back. For special discussions and problem solving you might want to make notes to remind yourself of important points.

How well do you and your friends communicate? Do you:

Choose appropriate words.

Accompany those words with loving actions?

Understand what is said and felt?

Keep on talking until both are satisfied?

Read On: Chapter 3, "Disappointments," and Chapter 4, "Conflicts," also contain communication ideas.

6
Honesty: The Courage to Be Myself

The Courage to Build a Friendship

"My mom grounded me from dating for a whole month! I'll die if I can't see Patrick!" said Jessica.

"Oh, how awful! Why don't you come spend the night at my house Friday and we can do something to take your mind off it?" invited Marla.

"That's a great idea!" said Jessica enthusiastically. "I can go out with Patrick and my mom will never know."

"That's not really what I had in mind," said Marla, hesitantly. "I feel terrible about your not being able to go out with Patrick, but I don't feel right about deceiving your mom."

"I thought you were my friend!" stormed Jessica as she slammed down the phone.

Who was being a friend? Why?

Was either girl being unfair to the other? How?

What would you have done in Marla's place? In Jessica's place?

Do What I Say and I'll Like You

Friendship is more than doing what our friends want us to do. Friendship must include such qualities such as:
honesty,
risk,

respect,
acceptance,
support, and
following our convictions.

Friendships die without them.

We believe this is true, yet few of us express these qualities in our friendships. Instead, we spend our time striving to please our friends and expecting them to please us. Why? We want our friends to like us. If we do what they want us to do, we feel that they will like us. And if they agree to our requests, we feel they care about us.

Friendships which are based on the you-do-what-I-want-and-I'll-like-you concept don't last long. Even while they last, they are not much fun. We hesitate to express our real feelings or beliefs for fear that our friends will not approve. Our friends learn to love the image we project and not the real us. We can never truly gain love if we pretend to be someone we're not.

Courage to try better techniques for making friends comes when we realize that pleasing our friends doesn't keep them for long. This courage comes gradually, and with God's help. It comes as we succeed at making new friends, as we discover that people really like us.

So how can we find this love we crave? How can we gain genuine love from our friends and show our love for them?

Try Some Better Ways

Honesty

Honesty sounds boring and isn't popular as a movie plot. But youth cite it as the number one characteristic needed for good friendship. They say dishonesty, lying, and deception quickly ruin friendships.

If we crave honesty, why is it so difficult?

We want honesty, but when we don't like what our friends

tell us, it's not easy to take. Jessica was honest with Marla by telling her that she wanted to go out with Patrick. Marla was honest by explaining that she could not honor Jessica's request. Jessica did not want this kind of honesty because it was inconvenient for her.

Risk

Marla risked (and received) Jessica's rejection by expressing her true feelings. Later, Jessica may respect and accept Marla, or she may not. But Marla can accept herself. Honesty is not always popular, convenient, or easy, but it builds strong relationships. This reward is worth the risk.

Respect

Love people and use things. Don't use people and love things. Jessica tried to use Marla to get what she wanted. She may not have deliberately put Marla into an uncomfortable position, but the results were the same. She failed to consider Marla, her thoughts, and her convictions.

A good friend cares about her friend's needs as well as her own needs.

Support

Each of us needs the support of our friends. Marla expressed her sympathy for Jessica's situation. She offered her emotional support and a listening ear. But Jessica would not accept this type of support. Jessica's idea of support was to be helped out of her mess. This view encouraged Jessica to work toward getting what she wanted rather than toward solving the situation.

Learn from Differences

Friends can learn from their differences. Jessica was eager to get what she wanted even if it meant being dishonest or using her friends. Marla felt that honesty would solve the problem more effectively, even if it meant difficulty in the present.

This difference is a major one. It is impossible for Jessica and Marla to agree as long as both remain firm in their positions. Agreement becomes possible only when one changes. Jessica might realize that honesty really does make things more comfortable in the long run. But, Marla might learn the unfortunate lesson of compromising her values to please a friend. Marla's change would be unhealthy for both girls.

Follow Your Convictions

The Jessica/Marla type of difference signals danger. But not all differences are bad. Positive differences make friendships interesting and colorful.

Joe likes Mexican food. Gary prefers hamburgers. Each decides to occasionally eat the other's food and learns to like it.

Teresa's idea of fun is a big party with plenty of music. Andi prefers long talks with one or two friends. Both Teresa and Andi try the other's favorite entertainment once in a while.

In Victor's family the conversation is loud and stormy. Disagreements are voiced firmly and forcefully. Amelia's home conversation is quieter. Each family member expresses opinions hesitantly, not wanting to hurt the other's feelings. Victor can learn from Amelia to listen and be sensitive. Amelia can learn from Victor the freedom to express her disagreement.

What makes these differences positive? Both members of the friendship can understand, accept, and enjoy the other's action or attitude without compromising their own commitments and values. The differences enrich rather than divide. They are based on opinion, not right and wrong.

Our Craving for Acceptance

We and our friends desperately need to be accepted. The main reason it is difficult to stand up for our convictions in friendship is this need for acceptance. We worry that our friends will quit liking us if we speak or act differently than they do.

We Need Acceptance

Risking rejection by a friend is not easy. When rejection comes you feel hurt and disappointed. And that's OK. We've all felt that way. But be assured that compromising your beliefs is not a path to acceptance. Friends would be accepting an image, not you. It is much more comfortable to be accepted for yourself than for the person your friends want you to be. The more friends you find who genuinely accept you (and they are out there!), the easier it becomes to handle rejection by a few others.

They Need Acceptance

Our friends need acceptance, too. Acting on our convictions can result in refusing an action or attitude. Our friends may take this as rejection of them.

We must show that it is the actions, not the person that we reject. Such acceptance is not easy to communicate, but we must never give up trying.

Marla might do this for Jessica by sharing the reason her action is not acceptable. "I care for you. I just can't do that because the Bible says it's wrong to deceive. If your mom finds out, you'll be even worse off than before."

Marla then must show Jessica that she still cares by continuing to call her and do things with her. This can help Jessica understand that Marla rejects the one action, not Jessica.

Read On: Chapter 5, "Communication," gives more ideas on how to communicate conflicting views.

When to Accept Actions

Some actions and attitudes are matters of opinion only. These differences are acceptable. Other differences are caused by one person obeying God and one disobeying Him. Such wrong actions and attitudes cannot be accepted.

Sometimes we accept wrong actions and attitudes to keep from hurting our friends' feelings. But condoning wrong actually brings more pain. If Marla helps Jessica deceive her parents to get what she wants, Jessica might later deceive her boyfriends, her friends, even herself. Once begun and accepted, such a habit is difficult to break. It will destroy each of Jessica's relationships. It is kinder to talk with friends about their wrong actions than to let those actions destroy them.

Hint: You might be the one with a wrong action or attitude. Be open to caring friends who try to help you.

How do we know which actions to accept?

Actions we should not accept from our friends include:

- physical or emotional abuse,
- deception and dishonosty,
- refusal to listen to our point of view,
- destruction of people or property,
- refusal to consider your needs or wants,
- denial of Christ and His ways.

Other actions and attitudes can be matters of opinion.

These include:

- what to eat,
- what to wear,
- when to give gifts,
- type of music,
- how to exercise,
- choice of occupation.

Would God accept it? You can accept it.

Would God question or reject it? Be certain you do so.

"Accept one another, then, just as Christ accepted you, in order to bring praise to God" (Rom. 15:7, NIV).

7
Popularity: Being a Part of the Group

The Popularity Question

"I'd give anything to be popular. Then I know I'd always have friends and I'd be liked by the best people. Popular people really have it made."

Popularity doesn't mean instant friendship, but it certainly looks that way. Why do we crave it? We want to be liked and we think we'll find it by being "in."

Being "In"

Belonging to the "in" group usually means wearing the latest clothes, having a gorgeous face and body, being rich, and holding a position like cheerleader, football player, or student body president.

Only a few people make the cheerleading squad and the football team. What about the rest of us? We could try developing a beautiful body and wear the latest fashions. But the shape and size of bodies cannot always be changed. (Nor should they be! Beauty comes in all shapes!) Also, money for funding an "in" wardrobe does not come easily.

Gaining popularity by developing the "in" personality often works. By acting, talking, and dressing "in" you can get invited to the "right" parties and become friends with the "right" people. But instead of finding friends who like you, you'll end up with people who like your image. Once you build an image, you fear letting others know the person hiding behind it. What if they don't like who they see? You remain lonely because no one really knows you.

Is there a solution to this problem? Yes:

When young people were asked what they wanted in a friend, no one mentioned anything about looks or clothes or popularity.

In fact, friendship destroyers, such as

dishonesty
lying
mistrust
competition
jealousy
peer pressure
and
lack of communication

are practiced daily by we who hide behind fashions and fads.

The solution begins by realizing that being "in" seldom gives us the friends we need. Being "liked" does.

Being Liked

"He's a user."

"She's two-faced."

"She says one thing and does another."

"He never hears a word I say."

Love doesn't come through designer clothes or a pretty face or an attractive body. Love, honesty, acceptance, and understanding come from inside.

"I've heard about the superior value of inner beauty all my life. But how can I feel this truth and relax enough to practice it?"

1. Realize that the "in" group is only one of many groups. It

seems like the only acceptable group of friends because it is the most visible one.

2. Understand that the struggle for popularity is one we all fight. You can win over the pressure to be popular.

3. Know that the popular group is not always the one which will make you happiest. Many popular people are lonely and miserable.

4. Believe that feeling incompetent or ugly or clumsy around certain people does not mean that you are incompetent, ugly, or clumsy. (Read about Sonya in Chapter 2).

5. Find a group that meets your needs and to which you can contribute. This group can help you like yourself.

6. Pray, pray, and pray some more: "Lord, help me to feel confident in the qualities you have given me. Assure me that I'm special. Give me comfort even around the people who make me feel ugly, dumb, or rejected."

Stop and Think: Remember—being *like* others does not equal being *liked* by them.

What's a Good Group?

If I'm not in the "in" group, how do I find a group I like? you ask.

Friends are essential. God knows how much we love and need our friends. He wants us to be in a group of friends we feel at home with. But not just any group will do. God wants the best for us. Good groups, like good friendships, must include:

- give and take
- mutual interest
- acceptance
- encouragement
- honesty
- communication
- loyalty
- commitment
- trust
- support
- expressed love
- enjoyment

Unfortunately, some groups make us unhappy or cause us to act in ways we know are wrong. Others keep us around only when we benefit them and desert us when we need them.

How can we be sure we choose a group that will be helpful

and supportive of us? Which groups are enjoyable? Which are painful?

Choosing a Good Group

Consider the advantages of a good group. Choose from the following list, the ones that are important to you.

- a feeling of belonging
- people to do something with
- a feeling of importance
- friends with whom to discuss problems
- a group in which to find a girl friend/boyfriend
- people who will encourage me to live Christianity
- friends who will stand up for me
- people who will encourage me to do what is right
- friends to help me decide what/who to like and do
- people who will like me just as I am
- a group with a reputation I can be proud of
- friends who welcome new people
- a group my parents like

The more advantages your group provides, the better. Be certain your group's advantages outweigh its disadvantages.

Let Me Be Me

I'm confused on one point. You say I should choose a group that encourages me to to be myself. I'm not sure who "myself" is. I often act one way around my school friends, another way around my church friends, and still another way around my family. Which is the real me?

Your question is a good one. The answer is difficult, partly because each of us is constantly "becoming." You gradually grow into the person you are.

Instead of, "Can I be myself?" try asking, "Does this group bring out qualities in me that I like?"

Which characteristics does your group bring out in you?

- easy to talk to
- good at ___
- patient
- good listener
- makes others comfortable
- honest
- good reputation
- sees the good in people

- two-faced
- uses people
- irritable
- snobbish
- critical
- sarcastic
- self-centered
- conceited

Do It Our Way

I think all this peer pressure is overblown. Friends don't make you do anything. I do what I want to do!

True, you make up your own mind and no group can tell you how to do that. But, pressure from others exists. How do you feel when you walk in a room wearing dress clothes when all the others are wearing jeans? Wouldn't you do almost anything to keep from feeling out of place?

That's the nature of peer pressure—a low key effort to be accepted by doing what others do. We think that being "like" our friends means being "liked" by them. We all know with our brains that being just like everyone else doesn't make us likable. But our emotions tell us otherwise. Because this subtle pressure to be like our friends is always present, it is important to choose a group that possesses the characteristics we want and that "pressures" us to be like Christ. We do become like the people we are around. Find "positive peer pressure!"

What behavior does your group encourage? If one member is not supposed to ride in a car with someone under seventeen, does the group dare her to ride with the sixteen-year-old anyway? If you finally find the courage to resist cheating, does your group encourage you or mock you?

Read On: 1 Corinthians 15:33 states, "Do not be fooled. "Bad companions ruin good character." "

Stop and Think: Why do you think we become like the people we are around? What qualities do your friends live?

But What Can I Do?

My group has more disadvantages than advantages. We tend to be cliquish; they laugh if I refuse to do something I think is wrong, and I'm afraid to express my Christianity. I don't want to hurt their feelings by pulling out. What if I don't find any other friends?

Leaving a group can be hard, but staying in a bad group is even harder. Concentrating on the advantages of another group can help make your transition easier.

Sometimes we fear that we'll never find another group. We stay with a destructive group because we think no one else will like us. But other groups exist and they will like you. Ask God to give you the courage to find them.

Make the change gradual. There are two steps: leaving your "old" group, and finding another.

Begin to select the activities you attend with your current group. If their plans include something you know is wrong, make other plans for that night. Your choice might give someone else in the group the courage they need.

To find another group, become friends with someone who expresses more of the characteristics you need. Soon this person may invite you along to his group activities. As you are busy with other things, you will gradually have less and less time to spend with your "old" group.

Christian Group?

"I hear a lot about choosing Christian friends. If we are

supposed to witness, it seems that we should be around non-Christians sometime!"

You are right that we need to be among non-Christian people, at least occasionally. "You are like salt for all mankind. . . . You are like light for the whole world" (Matt. 5:13, 14).

The key to this dilemma is twofold:

First, a non-Christian group must not be our only group. We need the support and encouragement of Christian friends as we struggle to obey Christ in everyday living (Heb. 10:24-25). But spending time with Christians only gives no opportunity to witness.

Second, it's sometimes hard to tell who is affecting whom. Does your presence stimulate your friends to consider Christ or do they make you hide your Christianity? (Ask an adult friend to help you decide.) Non-Christian friends can draw you away from God without your realizing it. Or, your Christian influence might interest them in God.

Into which category does your group fit:

A. Most members are actively involved in a church and daily try to live as Christians.

B. Some members go to church, but they don't really care how they live during the week.

C. Most members do not go to church or express Christian values, but they don't mind if I do.

D. Most members criticize my commitment to Christ.

The A category is the ideal, and the D category should definitely be avoided as a steady diet. It is possible you could be a positive influence on the B and C groups.

I ran around with a "C" group in high school. Most of the things we did as a group did not go against God, but some did. There was no drinking or drugs at our parties and we had good fun. My friends did not criticize my Christian commitment but didn't encourage it either.

Fay is fortunate that this group's indifference to Christianity did not cause her to become disinterested. This is probably because they were not her only group. Her involvement with Christian friends at church gave her the encouragement she needed to live her faith. The Christian life is not always easy. We need all the help we can get!

In deciding whether to be a member of a non-Christian group, consider two questions:

(1) "Am I receiving Christian fellowship somewhere?"

(2) "Am I influencing my non-Christian friends for Christianity or are they drawing me away from it?"

Cliques

"I don't mind groups of friends but I hate the cliques! They refuse to let new people in and have their own private activites and stories. What can I do about them?"

Cliques happen for several reasons.

Accident: Most youth genuinely do not want to exclude others. Knowing how horrible it feels, they wouldn't want to make anyone that miserable. But they get so wrapped up in their own friendships, they don't notice others. Though their exclusion is not deliberate, it is just as painful.

Security: Being accepted by a group feels comfortable. Often members will do nothing that jeopardizes their acceptance, including bringing in someone new. "What would they say if I became friends with Fred?" This cliquishness is based on the fear of rejection. Rather than risk being rejected themselves, such youth reject others.

Shyness: Few people meet new friends easily. We concentrate on the same comfortable chums. This comes across to outsiders as snobbishness. Most snobbish people are simply shy. Shy people are preoccupied with whether people like them.

When they find a few friends who care, they stay with them and refuse to risk meeting anyone new.

Common Interest: Football players naturally congregate because they understand each other and have much in common. It's troublesome to explain plays to someone ignorant of football jargon. It's easier to let that person find his own friends somewhere else. It may be easy for the football players, but it's not easy for the rejected person.

Personal Conflicts: When Frances stole Cassie's boyfriend, she started a vengeful rumor, causing the group to stop associating with Frances. Rather than dealing directly with their anger, Cassie used it to divide friendships and form a tighter clique.

Look back over these five reasons for cliques. They're all based on concern for one's own interests and comfort. A fancy word for this is "self-centeredness." Only when people reach beyond themselves, can they abolish cliques.

Forgetting your own needs to care for someone else is not easy. But it works. If you don't make friends with a person, chances are no one will. "Outsiders" are not the only ones who will profit from your friendliness: When you concentrate on others, you forget your own uneasiness.

What about you? Notice who you talk to. Is it always the same people or do you talk to those outside your closest circle of friends? Do you laugh about private jokes around those who don't understand? How easy is it to bring someone to a party who is not in your group?

Remember: A good group is great. But cliquishness takes away some of the greatness. Be certain your group actively welcomes new people.

Read On: Some Bible promises to help you handle the pressures to be popular are: 1 Peter 3:4; Philippians 4:13; Galatians 6:3.

8
Helping: My Friend Has a Problem

How to Help a Friend

Warren comes to me whenever he has a problem. I'm honored that he chooses me. He says I already understand him and he'd rather talk with me than some counselor.

When trouble strikes, people go first to a friend. Friends are chosen because of the care and trust already present in your friendship. But caring is not enough. You must know how to help. Knowing how to help can keep you from doing more harm than good.

When asked how they help their friends, people said:

"I listen."

"I try to put myself in her situation and imagine what I would do if I were in her position. Then tell her my ideas."

"I try to let her know that I'm willing to listen if she wants to talk about it and help her solve it if she wants."

"I talk with him and cry or laugh with him. We seek out an adult friend if it's a big problem. I follow up on the situation. I don't just talk once and expect it to go away."

"You don't really need to give advice unless they ask for it. Just give them someone to talk to."

"I let them know I'm there. If they share, I try to do what's in their best interest. I put my feelings aside."

Specific ways to do as suggested above are outlined in five situations: friends not around when you need them, jealousy, negative influence, family problems, and grief. The same helping techniques work for most other problems.

No Longer Time for Each Other

Ever since Cindie began going out with Wesley, she has had little time for you. She's no longer around to go shopping, to talk over problems, or to sit with. You really don't blame her because you'd like a boyfriend, too. But it seems she should be able to find time for friends.

"A friend means well, even when he hurts you" (Prov. 27:6). You don't feel like being friends with Cindie. She ignores you. Isn't it only fair that you ignore her in return? Maybe it's fair but it won't solve the problem.

Talking directly about friendship problems is hard, but helpful. Cindie may not realize she's neglecting you. She may not know how you feel.

There's a popular myth that says: "If she cared, she'd know how I feel. I shouldn't have to tell her." Friendships never outgrow the need for talking. We must share how we feel and need, or our friends may never know.

Tell Cindie you have something important to discuss. Find a good time to talk. Begin the conversation,

"I've really missed our long talks and doing stuff with you. I know your relationship with Wesley takes up most of your time, but could we plan to get together once a week or so? I'd like to hear how things are going with Wesley and I really need your ideas on what's happening in my life."

Cindie may respond in one or more of these ways:

Defensively: "You're just jealous because you don't have a boyfriend!"

Apologetic: "I guess I have been spending almost all my time with Wesley. I never meant to neglect you. I wouldn't hurt you for anything. Please forgive me!"

Cooperative: "I was so excited about Wesley I was ignoring my best friend! I never realized I was doing it! Of course we can get together! I've missed our talks."

Practice how you'd respond to each of these. Remain as calm as possible and express yourself honestly. This becomes easier by putting yourself in Cindie's position.

In the Shadow of a Star

Julian was inducted into the National Honor Society last week. He is calling to say that he has been offered scholarships from two colleges and doesn't know which one to take. Because you are having trouble even getting into college, it's hard to sympathize with his situation.

"Be happy with those who are happy, weep with those who weep" (Rom. 12:15). When a friend is receiving honors, high grades, or many invitations, we sometimes feel jealous instead of happy. This is normal. Instead of feeling bad about it, admit it, and move on to more positive feelings.

You might say, "I know your decision is hard but I must say that I'm a wee bit jealous. I've never been offered one scholarship, let alone two! If I act funny, it's not that I don't care, I just don't know what to say!"

Being honest like this is hard, but helps to clear away frustration. Take a moment to privately point out to yourself the things you do well—you may not excel in school, but you make friends easily; you are a good listener; or you make great chocolate chip cookies.

Then help your friend decide by asking such helping questions as:

- What do the two colleges offer?

• What are the advantages/disadvantages of each choice?
• What advice do you think Jesus would give?
• Which school offers more of the courses, location, and future possibilities that you want?

Bad Company

Anna's boyfriend is of the wilder type. Everyone tried to warn her when they began dating, but she felt she could be a good influence on him. After all, he never did bad stuff when she was around. But last week when they were out together, he broke into a house and stole some jewelry. Anna just called to say that the police found her fingerprints along with his.

"Do not be fooled. "Bad companions ruin good character" " (1 Cor. 15:33). When such trouble strikes our friends, we are unsure how to respond. Because we don't know what to say or do, we often avoid our friends. This comes across as rejection or desertion. Though it's true that Anna has let herself be negatively influenced by her boyfriend, it is not time to desert her. She needs the positive care of friends.

What can you say to Anna? Will your parents forbid you to see her because of the trouble she's in? How will being her friend affect you? How can you be sure you will affect her positively rather than she affect you negatively?

The answers to these questions are not easy. But there are some principles that can bring positive results.

1. *Listen and ask questions.* Because you do not know exactly what is best, nor can you change what has happened, help Anna solve her own problem.

Listen to her feelings and her words. Ask such questions as: "How do you feel about that?" "What do you think will happen if you try it?" "What do you think God wants you to do?"

2. *Assure her of your continued care.* This does not mean to approve of what she does. It means you won't reject her when she makes a mistake. You know you care, but Anna may doubt

it. Show it by sitting with her at church and school functions, by sending cards, by talking.

3. *Notice the good as well as the bad.* Anna has stolen something, but she is still a good student. Ask about that part of her life, too. Noticing and complimenting the good may give Anna the courage to overcome her problems instead of repeating them.

4. *Watch your own actions.* When being around Anna encourages you to do wrong, she's influencing you negatively. If this happens, spend less time with her.

5. *Call for adult help.* Ministers, counselors, and other adults care about youth problems. Anna's situation is one too big for most youth to handle alone. Adults can help you help. Don't hesitate to let them.

6. *Take seriously your parents' words.* Parents can suggest ways to help or notice her influence on you. Even when they seem wrong, listen to what they are say and why.

Pain at Home

"They were such a good Christian couple! Who would've thought it would happen to them, . . ." you overhear your parents say. They're talking about Ron's parents. Ron has been angry and withdrawn since his parents' divorce. You don't know what to say to him.

"Friends always show their love. What are brothers for if not to share trouble" (Prov. 17:17)? Divorce is never easy for the parents or the children. You can help Ron by understanding him.

Ron may feel:

Angry at his parents for divorcing.

Confused over which parent to live with.

Embarrassed to be the son of divorced parents.

Uncertain of his parents' love for him.

Ron may worry that:

People won't like him because his parents are divorced.
He caused the divorce.
He must choose between parents.
His parents will "divorce" him.

Though you may not have been through divorce, you have felt:

angry
confused
embarrassed
uncertain

You have worried that:

people might not like you
you are responsible for someone else's actions
you must make a hard choice
people will reject you

Because you know Ron's feelings you can more easily understand him. Ron's anger and withdrawal are attempts to protect himself from further pain.

Try such words as:

"I want you to know I care."
"What thoughts have you had about your folks' divorce?"
"How are you feeling?"
"How are things going at school, church, home?"
"Feel free to call me anytime."

Ron may express anger toward you. He may not welcome your care. But gently express it anyway. In time, he'll be able to accept it.

Dealing with Doubt

Janice and you talk about God often. When her dad died suddenly, Janice lashed out at you and at God, "Why would a loving God let this happen to my dad?" You wonder what to say to her when you see her tomorrow.

"A gentle answer quiets anger, but a harsh one stirs it up" (Prov. 15:1). Death, doubt, and anger are especially tough problems. We'd rather not deal with them. But avoidance brings more pain. Sad friends need more loving, not less.

1. *Accept grief as normal and necessary.* Shock, profuse emotion, anger at God or the doctors, depression, and eventual acceptance are stages in every person's grief.

2. *Listen.* Janice needs to tell someone the feelings that make her miserable. Don't change the subject when her dad's death comes up.

3. *Show understanding.* Understanding words coupled with hugs, smiles, and genuineness show you understand.

"I can see why you'd be angry at God; it seems like He doesn't care. He does, but it's hard to feel it now."

4. *Keep in touch.* Losing someone by death may take a long time—months, even years—to adjust to. This grief process is made easier by a steady friend. Send cards. Go places together. Talk. Do the friend things that have always been special to you.

5. *Ask an adult friend to help you understand the grief process.* You'll know what to expect and how to help.

Advice About Giving Advice

Giving advice is easy and can show concern. But be aware of a significant danger: Your advice may be wrong.

Advice giving has benefits and dangers. Some are:

Benefits	Dangers
Your friend may not know what to do.	What worked for you may not work for your friends.
Advice given well can help a person solve his own problem.	Your friend may depend on you to solve all his problems and never do it alone.
God's advice works for everyone. If we hear His advice right, we'll give His	Even though God's advice always works, only God knows which advice best fits each

advice. We can feel confident sharing it.

Your friend may need ideas on how to solve his problem.

situation. The guidance may be best left to Him.

Your friend may blame you if your advice doesn't work.

Your advice may be right. Your advice may be wrong.

Given the dangers of advice giving, it is usually more effective to guide your friend to make a personal decision than to do the friend's thinking for him. Do this by listening, asking questions, listing, and evaluating possible solutions. Letting your friend solve his own problem is effective because he knows his situation best. Also, he will more likely follow a solution he thought of himself.

Conquering Your Friendship Problems

Cindie, Julian, Anna, Ron, and Janice represent a few of the many problems that confront friendship. The methods that helped them are summarized in "H-E-L-P F-R-I-E-N-D-S."

H-elp your friend solve his problem himself.
E-mpathize—Understand thoughts and worries.
L-isten and ask questions.
P-ut yourself in your friend's situation.
F-ocus on the reasons behind the problem.
R-ealize that problems come to all friendships.
I-nformation—find and use it.
E-nlist the help of caring adults.
N-otice feelings, yours and your friend's.
D-iscuss problems directly.
S-ee that your friend does most of the talking.

Read On: Biblical quidelines for solving friendship problems include: Galatians 6:1-2; Philippians 2:4; 1 Corinthians 10:13; 2 Corinthians 1:3-4; Hebrews 10:24-25.

9
Sweethearts: Becoming More than Friends

"I don't want to date you. I just want to be your friend," said Willis. Pam knew this meant the end. What Willis really meant was, "I want to date Sandy."

"It is so great to have guys for friends!" said Tracy. "You don't have to worry about putting on a big front like when you're out on a date."

Are friends and sweethearts two different breeds? Not necessarily. The best boyfriend or girl friend must first be a friend. Though it's extremely difficult to keep your emotions in check long enough to become friends, a friendship base makes a stronger romantic relationship.

Friendship Facts

Making friends with the opposite sex is a lot like making friends with the same sex. Friends are people first and then males or females. Let's review two principles:

Friend Making Is a Process

Neither friendship nor romance happen instantly, like in the movies. The funny feeling in your stomach may mean you are in love but may also mean that your supper did not agree with you. Friendship is romantic and exciting but is just as often frustrating, confusing, and plain hard work. This work involves talking, sharing feelings, listening, and working out problems. This work helps love last even when romantic feelings are absent.

Friendships Grow Constantly

Friends grow together or apart. Friends grow together by continually learning to better understand each other, to talk, to solve problems, to make each other happy, and to enjoy life. Friends who grow apart neglect these tasks.

Friendship Skills

Skills you'll want in your male/female friendship are:

• *Listening:* Listening is more than just closing the mouth (even though this is hard for some of us!). It's hearing and understanding what the other is saying and feeling. Instead of worrying about what you are going to say back, be challenged to discover what your friend is telling you. Does he need celebration, reassurance, ideas, sympathy, encouragement, or simply listening ears? Silently count to ten before responding to insure your friend is finished.

• *Genuineness:* Impressing is important in the beginning. But keeping it up continuously results in a tight stomach, not a tight relationship. As you try being genuine and are accepted for it, you will have courage to try again. The more you find acceptance, the less you'll fear rejection.

• *Acceptance:* In order for honest sharing to happen, we must accept our friends. This does not mean we tolerate every action, but that we accept the person.

Unconditional acceptance can be tricky. We all know of the girl who puts up with garbage from her boyfriend because "that's just the way he is." She is failing to respect herself. She can communicate her need without rejecting her friend by saying, "It really hurts me when you do that."

A better example of unconditional acceptance is the friend

who forgives without keeping a "record of wrongs" (see 1 Cor. 13:4-7).

Esther just lost her temper again. She feels depressed about it. Andy reassures her of his support as she learns to manage her anger.

• *Sensitivity.* Has your friend had a bad day? Notice. Refrain from sharing your good news until she can share her frustrations. Is your friend wanting to tell you something, but hesitating? Try to be a little quieter or ask: "Is something on your mind? Do you want to talk?"

The above four skills combine to form communication.

The more subjects you can talk about,
the more openly you can talk about them,
and the better you understand one another when you do talk,
the stronger your friendship will be.

How to Get to Know a Friend of the Opposite Sex Better

Experiences together are a key to growing a friendship. The more time you spend together and the more different ways you spend your together time, the stronger your friendship will grow.

Share a Variety of Activities

Try some of these with your friend:

Take a walk.
Talk about a problem.
Mow the lawn.
Shop for a gift together.
Get together with other friends.
Watch a TV show and talk about it.
Baby-sit for your cousins.
Play sports.
Read a Bible passage.
Paint for a neighbor.
Clean the kitchen.
Do exercises.
Cook a meal.
Teach a Bible study.

Male/female pairs who spend their time only on such formal things as going to movies, will know little about how they relate in everyday happenings:

- What does she do when she's mad?
- How does he handle disappointment?
- How well does she handle responsibility?
- How does he manage his time?
- How do children respond to her?
- How does he handle conflict?
- What does she do in her free time?
- What does he do around the house?

The answers to these and more questions can be found only through spending time in a variety of situations.

Stop and Think: Which activities could give you the answers to each of the above questions?

Watch How Sweethearts Relate to Others

Spend time with groups and as a twosome. Both help to develop your relationship. Watching how your sweetheart relates to people besides you tells you a great deal.

Dale constantly criticized others, both in their presence and behind their back. He never criticized Grace, but she wondered what he said when she was not around.

Betty Anne could make others comfortable. She seemed to help shy people to talk. Sad folk smiled when she came in the room. Tony was proud to have such a caring girl friend.

Roxanne was the class clown. In a crowd she was always telling jokes and acting foolish. Bart enjoyed her antics but wished she would be serious, at least occasionally.

Stop and Think: How does your "opposite sex" friend act in a group? What does this tell you about him/her?

Values/Advantages/Pleasures

What are the advantages of male/female relationships? Following are just a few. I know you can add to the list:

It prepares you for marriage. The one you marry becomes your lifelong best friend. Romance and gushy feelings are fun but they don't hold a marriage together. Most of marriage time is spent sharing routine daily tasks with someone you like. This brings tremendous enjoyment.

It teaches you how to relate to the opposite sex. To enjoy routine daily life with someone, you have to know how to talk to, listen to, and enjoy one another. Friendship is great practice.

Male/female friendships often bring less worry and more pleasure than dating relationships. You might find yourself growing to love romantically your opposite sex friend simply because you were relaxed enough to get to know one another.

The opposite sex can help with dating problems. I don't think that men and women are much different on the basic issues, but sometimes guys think and act differently than girls and vice versa. Guy friends can explain guy actions and vice versa.

Friendships don't usually "break up." Male/female friendships often last longer than romances. If friends grow apart, it is usually more gradual and less painful than the end of a dating relationship.

Disadvantages/Frustrations/Pain

There are some frustrations to male/female friendships. Knowing what these are can help you deal with them.

You might want to be "more than friends." The words we never want to hear from someone we're dating are "let's be friends." That usually means they want out of the romance relationship. On the other hand, we ourselves might want to be friends but the other person wants more.

Stop and Think: How have you handled this problem?

Dating can complicate the friendship. Both of you may decide you want "more" than friendship and you begin to date. If one of you discovers that you really do not want to be that close, it is often difficult to go back to "being friends." Many find it impossible.

Normal friendship problems come. Problems such as disagreement, disappointment, misunderstanding, and pain are definitely a part of male/female friendship. Knowing that these problems come to every relationship, can free you to fight them instead of worry about them.

Intimacy and Friendship

Intimacy is a fancy word for "being close." Total intimacy means being able to reveal everything about yourself to another. This includes the mental, emotional, spiritual, and physical dimensions. Of course, the only total intimacy is the marriage relationship.

Intimacy is not something you have or don't have. All relationships have some level of intimacy in one or more of the dimensions. We have non-Christian friends with whom we have no spiritual intimacy. We have friends with whom we share spiritually, but not mentally/emotionally.

Male/female friendships include mental, emotional, and spiritual intimacy with limited amounts of physical intimacy. Physical intimacy is rightly limited to friendly hugs. Kissing and holding hands are left to dating.

Quality physical intimacy depends on good mental, emotional, and spiritual intimacy. You must be able to talk to and understand each other before you can be truly close. Relationships based on physical intimacy alone are doomed to fail. Physical affection is not strong enough to hold a relationship together. Male/female friendships teach us how to be intimate mentally, emotionally, and spiritually without potentially explosive physical intimacy.

What's the Difference?

So what's the difference between friendship and dating? Sometimes that line is difficult to draw. Friendships usually do not include physical intimacy or "romance."

And, yet, romance can be a myth. The happiest friendships are built on sincere sharing and hard work, not gushy feelings. Because the best romance is built on good friendship, the best sweetheart is a good friend. How do you know if your friend is a sweetheart? Wait and see which the relationship grows toward. In the meantime, enjoy yourself!

Some Letters on Specifics

The responses to these letters from youth contain ideas which may help you deal with similar problems.

I'm crazy about Dave. We've been dating about a year. I love his gentle charm and teasing ways. He is deeply committed to Christ and that's so important to me. My feelings for him are serious but he is not ready for a steady relationship. He insists that he wants to date but not "get serious." I keep hoping he'll change and like me more, but I remain disappointed. What should I do?

A good way to attack this sensitive problem is to talk about it. Be open with each other about how you see the relationship. If the difference is as you perceive, you may need to quit seeing one another. This sounds drastic, but continuing to date is simply too painful for the one who wants more than friendship. Each date gives you unfulfilled hope for deeper commitment.

Undoubtedly the problem also frustrates Dave. He may feel trapped or pressured. Closing the relationship, at least for a time, will help both of you sort out your emotions. Though you may not believe it, not seeing Dave will be easier than your current misery.

I tried to be nice to this girl in class and now she has a crush on me. She took my attention the wrong way! How can I tell her my feelings without making her feel bad?

This is a tough situation, but one which almost everyone experiences. First, take her affection as a compliment.

Second, understand there is no way to completely avoid pain. Though it may seem kinder to avoid the problem, her pain will be much less if you deal with the situation straightforwardly.

The more direct she is about her affection for you, the easier it is. If she is fairly open, you can talk with her about the confusion in your relationship. Be certain to be honest, to affirm her as a person, and to not say anything that might lead her on. Try, "I am complimented by your care for me. Because I care, I want to say I like you as a friend, not a sweetheart. I'm sorry I communicated my friend love in the wrong way. I value you as a friend and don't want to hurt you worse by leading you on."

Because you and she will probably be embarrassed by this conversation, talk when there will be time to "recover" afterwards. Don't talk right before a big test or an outing.

If you can "just tell" she likes you, you have a more difficult problem.

- Caring in a group often helps. The less you are alone together, the less she will take your care as romance.
- Enlist female friends to befriend her. The more she is loved by others, the less she needs to depend on you.
- Do or say nothing that could be taken romantically. As time goes on and you have not asked her out or called her on the phone, she will gently begin to see her mistake.
- If she asks you out, respond with a firm, but gentle "no thank you." If she presses, say something like "I want to be friends but not date you."

All the guys see me as their dating counselor. It really hurts when a guy I like comes to me with his girl friend problem. How can I get them to notice me as more than a "big sister?"

Your problem does have its positives. You have an inside track into the way guys think. You are gaining great practice at problem solving and at being comfortable with guys. That's great preparation for "sweetheart-ness."

But your need for romance remains. Don't panic. It will come. In the meantime there are some things you can do in a relaxed way:

- Believe that you are likable. Your feeling about yourself is picked up by others and they believe it.
- Honest flirting: If you like a fellow romantically, let him know it. Many guys are afraid to ask girls out for fear of rejection. An appropriately timed smile or "I'm glad you're here" can hint of your affection.
- Pray. God cares a lot about this issue and can motivate the relationships He has in mind. Ask Him to bring you and the right boy(s) together, and to guide you to say and do the right things to make a relationship happen.

10
The End: When Friendships Change

Keeping a Good Thing Going

What keeps friendships close?

Most people agree that you cannot force a friendship. But you can and must nurture one or it will die. A good way to keep a friendship from dying is to take care of it when it is new and healthy. Do this through:

- regular contact,
- talking and sharing,
- listening,
- understanding,
- making memories,
- sharing special experiences.

Neglect Brings Unnecessary Deaths

If you don't want to bother keeping your friendships alive, they will die by neglect. To kill a friendship:

- spend little time together.
- forget most of the things your friend tells you.
- frequently fail to understand.
- criticize each other constantly.
- forget to compliment.
- take your bad moods out on your friends.
- say whatever you feel, no matter its effects.

- refuse to apologize.
- consider only your own wants and needs.
- make your friend do all the calling and inviting.
- refuse to keep in touch—by letter, phone, or visit.

Changes Still Come

No matter what you may do to nurture your friendship, changes still come. You feel closer to some people than you did last year. Others who were close last year seem like strangers. Why are things so different?

Friendships change constantly. They either grow together or they grow apart.

Changes in friendship can be temporarary or permanent, painful or easy, sudden or gradual. Friends can often grow along with changes. Other times, the friendship ends. What causes friendship changes?

You
Conflicts
Circumstances
New Friends
Sweethearts
Miscommunication

Changes in You

Because you change, your friendships change. Your personality, preferences, and interests grow constantly into what you and God want them to be. As you grow, you try out ideas, learn the best values, and understand how to apply God's truths to your life. The changes brought by this growth can be both exciting and difficult. These changes are one reason the teen years are full of emotion. The confusion and uncertainty you experience happen to all youth. Life will become more steady as you grow older.

Penny and her friends loved to go shopping. They read extensively on the latest fashions and built their wardrobes accordingly. But as Penny's confidence grew, she had less interest in clothes. She wanted to look attractive, but realized that people liked her, not her clothes. Consequently, the shopping trips became less important. Because this had been the basis of their friendship, Penny and her friends grew apart.

Jason returned from his first sememster of college bursting with excitement. He and his high school buddies gathered for a night out. But Jason felt funny. They no longer had as much in common. His dad said it was normal to grow in different directions during college. It had happened to him. He advised them to enjoy one another when together, but to understand that they might not feel as close.

Growing less close does not mean that the friendship was not important or good. Once a person has been your friend, he will always remain special. You may not do as much together, but you will still be important to one another.

Conflict

Conflict comes to all friendships. Most can be resolved. Some must be worked around.

Tina loved card games. As she grew closer to Tad, she discovered that he took card games too seriously. He sulked when he lost, was militant about rules, and stole all the joy from the game. Tina decided not to play cards with Tad. The two found other pleasures they could enjoy.

Others can destroy a relationship.

Irene refused to talk when something bothered her. She felt that problems were bad and talking about them was worse.

Elaine rightly felt that problems could be ended by talking them out. No matter how much Elaine encouraged her, Irene refused to discuss angry feelings. This made Elaine miserable. She was compelled to find friends who deal with problems directly rather than burying them alive. Elaine maintained occasional contact with Irene but Irene's silence kept their friendship distant.

Read On: See the chapters on conflicts and communication for ideas on how to solve conflicts.

Circumstances

Trips,
a new school year,
a new commitment,
moving away,
greater maturity, and
other circumstances
change friendships.
Sometimes these changes bring added closeness.

When the new schedules arrived, Brenda discovered she had no classes with her current friends. She worried, "Will we still be close? Will I find friends in my new classes?" Brenda made new friends, but also discovered her first friends remained important. She maintained closeness through talking in the hall, church activities, and phone conversations. She gained confidence when she realized that her friends continued to like her.

Some changes bring separation:

Liz became a Christian at the retreat. She eagerly shared the news with her friends. But they responded coldly. "Now you won't be able to have fun anymore. Why did you do that?" Liz was crushed. Her friends did not understand Christianity. She tried to explain that God's fun was longer lasting and without hangovers. They wouldn't buy it. Liz gradually spent more time with her Christian friends, around whom she could be herself. She maintained contact with her non-Christian friends. One even became a Christian. But the group no longer accepted her.

Liz's change was definitely more difficult, but she handled it wisely. By developing friends who put her at ease, she was better able to handle the frustrations her former friends offered. She continued to accept them but said no thank you to some of their activities. She allowed the painful friendships to drift apart gradually.

New Friends

A childhood song goes:

Make new friends but keep the old,
One is silver and the other gold.

But there are times when new friends overshadow the old. The excitement of meeting and getting to know someone new may make already established friendships seem boring. All relationships have this exciting beginning and then settle down. The excitement part can be called "the romance of newness." Think of romance as that exhiliarating feeling that makes every experience feel great. You can experience that with a new friend as well as with a new sweetheart.

Don't Leave Them Behind

Your understanding of this truth can prevent you from hurting your current friends when a new friend comes along. There is room for more than one friend! Even the most exciting new friendship will settle to "normal." Long-lasting friendships have their own kind of excitement.

Because no friendship can maintain a constant high level of

excitement, remember to cultivate your current friendships as well as new ones. Do this by:

- Noticing your friend's good points.
- Trying something new.
- Writing "I like you because . . ." letters.
- Thinking what life might be like without her.
- Sharing dreams and hopes.

I'm Left Behind

What if you are the left-behind-friend? Your friend spends more time with the new friend than with you. She acts like she doesn't care about you or your feelings.

Expect pain. You will feel jealous, hurt, and sad. You may feel the new person is better than you. You may feel deserted.

Recognize your feelings. Talk them out with someone you trust. Pray that God will help you turn your jealousy into understanding and love. Jealousy is normal, but be certain you control it rather than letting it control you.

Talk gently but directly. "I'm sad that you've been spending so much time with Jodi. I need some time with you. Could we get together Friday?"

Wait. Remember the newness principle. The excitement of the new friendship will ease. Time for you will return.

Examine yourself. Was there something you did that caused the separation? Do you need to apologize? Can you stop a harmful attitude/action or begin a positive one?

Forgive your friend. Try to understand your friend's situation. He may or may not have meant to hurt you. Forgiving him in either case can cleanse the bitter feelings from you and free your friend to resume friendship with you.

Consider becoming friends with the new person. Remember what it felt like when you were new. Welcome her with the love you needed. If your friend likes her, you might, too!

Pray. Ask God to help you understand what He wants the

friendship to be. If He wants you to grow closer, do your part. If it's the end, pray for strength to let go.

Caution: Too many of us let our loyalty for our current friends become cliquishness. We refuse to welcome anyone new. This hurts new people, and also deprives us of potential friends. The song is true: we need both old and new friends.

Sweethearts

She has a boyfriend now and no longer has time for me. I wish I had a boyfriend. Maybe we'd have something in common again.

One friend has found a sweetheart and spends all her time with him. The same-sex friend is neglected, feels useless, and craves attention.

This problem is easy because:

- The separation is often temporary.
- Your friend still likes you. She's just preoccupied.
- You are happy for your friend.

But it is difficult because:

- It makes you aware of your desire for a sweetheart.
- You are still lonely.
- You sometimes feel like a fifth wheel.

As suggested in Chapter 8, "Helping," talking with your friend can return some of the friendship time you crave.

If you are the one with the sweetheart, reserve time for your same-sex friends. Gently help your sweetheart understand that though he is important to you, you need your friends, too. Suggest that your sweetheart spend time with his friends when you are with yours. Anyone, friend or sweetheart, who monopolizes your time is thinking more of himself than you.

Who is more important: a friend or a sweetheart? *Both.* If either is neglected for the sake of the other, no one wins. Find sweethearts and friends who will encourage your relationships with others, not stifle them.

Miscommunication

Some friends grow apart because they misunderstand what each other says and does.

After five years we're not best friends anymore. Colleen came right out and told me last Monday. She and Debra hung out together the whole week. I hung around Jay, but I felt so left out and lonely. The most painful part is that Colleen's not even worried about our friendship. Things have changed so much. It hurts so bad to lose someone you've been close to for five years.

This friendship is infested with miscommunication and mistaken assumptions.

What this person understood as the end of friendship may have been Colleen trying to say, "I need other friends, too." Misunderstandings like these stem from insecurities and fear that others don't like us. Talking them out helps. This single incident doesn't have to mean the end.

The friends were on a senior class trip when this event occurred. Adventures such as travel, a new romance, and a new school year can change feelings for awhile. Return to routine usually returns friends to one another.

Assumptions affect the way two friends relate to each other. *Assumption* is a fancy word for "the way I see things." If the friend assumes Colleen doesn't like her anymore, she may hesitate to call Coleen or to tell her special secrets. Colleen may assume this means "She's mad at me." Talking rather than assuming can save unnecessary pain.

What If My Friendship Spells D-A-N-G-E-R?

Most of the time friendship problems are worked out and we

adjust to changes. But occasionally the friendship must end. When a friendship is destructive to you, let it die.

This **DANGER** acrostic can help you remember some of the more frequent friendship destroyers.

D ishonesty
A nger unresolved (Anger is not bad; but work it out.)
N eglecting to express love and appreciation
G iving without getting or getting without giving
E ncouraging you to do wrong
R estrictiveness (Do it *my* way or else!)

Your friendship might be bringing you down instead of building you up, discouraging you, instead of encouraging you, bringing out the worst in you rather than the best. You might fight more than you enjoy each other. You might hesitate to live your beliefs or share your true feelings. You might feel used. What can you do?

It is painful to withdraw from any friendship, even an unhealthy one. But the pain is worse if you remain. Let the end be gradual. This gives you time to find other friends and to adjust to the changes.

- Improve the friendship where you can by using some of the friendship skills and problem-solving techniques discussed in this book.
- Build healthy friendships with others that can help you cope with this frustrating one.
- Gently back off from the friendship by doing less and less together. Be busy with other activities.

If a friendship dies, let it be because it is for the best, not because one or both of you refused to nurture the friendship or to give it the importance it deserved.

Hint: You may be the one contributing D-A-N-G-E-R to a friendship. Both bad friendship skills and good friendship skills are learned. It is not too late for you to learn positive friendship skills. Make a conscious effort to do so.

It Doesn't Have to Be the End

Good friendships are not always forever friendships. Certain people become important to us at certain times because of mutual interest or problems. Later we may drift apart.

Even parted friends can remain friends—not close friends, or best friends, but friends nonetheless. Once you have shared friendship, that person remains special.

It's Not that Simple

Parting friendship is a touchy issue. Our society emphasizes that it's OK to change replationships frequently.

"What we had was good while it lasted, but it's over."

"Easy come, easy go."

Friendships may be easy come, but they are seldom easy go. Be certain to do all you can to nurture and preserve the quality of each friendship you enter. Of course you won't be best friends with everyone, but you can promote a healthy and happy relationship. If and when your level of closeness changes, continue to care for the person.

You Can Make a Difference

If you notice yourself growing independent of a friend who still needs you, be sensitive. At times it is best to talk about it. Other times it is best to let the friendship drift gradually by doing less and less together.

The way you treat your friends can have life-changing effects. You can increase or devastate their confidence. You can help them feel good about themselves or hate themselves. You can encourage them to do good or to inflict pain. Your actions and attitudes toward friends make a difference. Make it a postive difference.

Read On: 1 Corinthians 13:4-8 describes God's kind of love. Strive to cultivate this love in your friendships.

Subject Index